20 best
boozy baking
recipes

Houghton Mifflin Harcourt
Boston • New York • 2013

Copyright © 2013 by General Mills, Minneapolis, Minnesota. All rights reserved.

For information about permission to reproduce selections from this book, write to Permissions, Houghton Mifflin Harcourt Publishing Company, 215 Park Avenue South, New York, New York 10003.

www.hmhco.com

Cover photo: Boozy Bourbon-Chocolate Cupcakes (page 16)

General Mills
Food Content and Relationship Marketing Director: Geoff Johnson
Food Content Marketing Manager: Susan Klobuchar
Senior Editor: Grace Wells
Kitchen Manager: Ann Stuart
Recipe Development and Testing: Betty Crocker Kitchens
Photography: General Mills Photography Studios and Image Library

Houghton Mifflin Harcourt
Publisher: Natalie Chapman
Editorial Director: Cindy Kitchel
Executive Editor: Anne Ficklen
Associate Editor: Heather Dabah
Managing Editor: Rebecca Springer
Production Editor: Kristi Hart
Cover Design: Chrissy Kurpeski
Book Design: Tai Blanche

ISBN 978-0-544-31467-2
Printed in the United States of America

The Betty Crocker Kitchens seal guarantees success in your kitchen. Every recipe has been tested in America's Most Trusted Kitchens™ to meet our high standards of reliability, easy preparation and great taste.

FIND MORE GREAT IDEAS AT
BettyCrocker.com

Dear Friends,

This new collection of colorful mini books has been put together with you in mind because we know that you love great recipes and enjoy cooking and baking but have a busy lifestyle. So every little book in the series contains just 20 recipes for you to treasure and enjoy. Plus, each book is a single subject designed in a bite-size format just for you—it's easy to use and is filled with favorite recipes from the Betty Crocker Kitchens!

All of the books are conveniently divided into short chapters so you can quickly find what you're looking for, and the beautiful photos throughout are sure to entice you into making the delicious recipes. In the series, you'll discover a fabulous array of recipes to spark your interest—from cookies, cupcakes and birthday cakes to party ideas for a variety of occasions. There's grilled foods, potluck favorites and even gluten-free recipes too.

You'll love the variety in these mini books—so pick one or choose them all for your cooking pleasure.

Enjoy and happy cooking!

Sincerely,

Betty Crocker

contents

Wine-derful Cakes

Zinfandel Wine Cupcakes · 7
Pink Champagne Layer Cake · 8
Lemon Champagne Celebration
  Cupcakes · 9
Chocolate-Fig Cake with Mascarpone
  Frosting · 10

Beer-licious Baking

Chocolate-Stout Caramel Corn · 11
Beer-and-Pretzel Chocolate
  Chip Cookies · 12
Triple Chocolate–Stout Whoopie Pies · 13
Tall, Dark and Stout Chocolate
  Layer Cake · 14
Salted Caramel, Stout and Chocolate
  Cheesecake · 15

Bourbon Desserts

Boozy Bourbon-Chocolate Cupcakes · 16
Pecan-Bourbon-Crunch Italian Cream
  Cups · 17
Chocolate-Bourbon Pumpkin
  Cheesecake · 18
Bourbon Brownie Bites with Dulce de
  Leche · 20
Bourbon–Pecan Pie with
  Pecan Crust · 21

Rum-Tastic Treats

Rum-Glazed Spice Cocktail Cookies · 22
Pecan-Rum Bars · 23
Mojito Cake · 24
Chocolate Rum Cake · 25
Hot Buttered Rum Cheesecake with
  Brown Sugar–Rum Sauce · 26
Pear-Rum Crisp · 27

Metric Conversion Guide · 29
Recipe Testing and Calculating
  Nutrition Information · 30

Wine-derful Cakes

Zinfandel Wine Cupcakes

Prep Time: 30 Minutes • **Start to Finish:** 1 Hour 35 Minutes • Makes 24 cupcakes

Cupcakes

1 box Betty Crocker® SuperMoist® devil's food cake mix

¾ cup water

½ cup Zinfandel wine

⅓ cup vegetable oil

3 eggs

1 cup miniature semisweet chocolate chips

Frosting

6 cups powdered sugar

⅓ cup butter, softened

⅓ cup unsweetened baking cocoa

⅛ teaspoon salt

½ cup Zinfandel wine

Garnish

Chocolate curls

1 Heat oven to 350°F (325°F for dark or nonstick pans). Place paper baking cup in each of 24 regular-size muffin cups.

2 In large bowl, beat cake mix, water, ½ cup wine, the oil and eggs with electric mixer on low speed 30 seconds. Beat on medium speed 2 minutes, scraping bowl occasionally. Stir in chocolate chips. Divide batter evenly among muffin cups, filling each about two-thirds full.

3 Bake 20 to 22 minutes or until toothpick inserted in center comes out clean. Cool 10 minutes; remove cupcakes from pans to cooling racks. Cool completely, about 30 minutes.

4 In large bowl, beat powdered sugar, butter, cocoa and salt with electric mixer on low speed until blended. Beat in ½ cup wine. If frosting is too thick, beat in more wine, a few drops at a time. Frost cupcakes. Garnish with chocolate curls.

1 Cupcake: Calories 290; Total Fat 9g (Saturated Fat 4g, Trans Fat 0g); Cholesterol 35mg; Sodium 190mg; Total Carbohydrate 50g (Dietary Fiber 1g); Protein 2g **Exchanges:** ½ Starch, 3 Other Carbohydrate, 1½ Fat **Carbohydrate Choices:** 3

Tip To make chocolate curls, warm a chocolate bar by holding it in your hands for several minutes until slightly softened. Using a vegetable peeler, shave the chocolate in long strands along the smooth side of the chocolate. Transfer the curls with a toothpick to the cupcakes.

Pink Champagne Layer Cake

Prep Time: 30 Minutes • **Start to Finish:** 2 Hours 15 Minutes • Makes 12 servings

Cake

1 box Betty Crocker Super-Moist white cake mix

1¼ cups champagne, room temperature

⅓ cup vegetable oil

3 egg whites

4 to 5 drops red food color

Frosting

½ cup butter, softened

4 cups powdered sugar

¼ cup champagne, room temperature

1 teaspoon vanilla

4 to 5 drops red food color

Garnishes, if desired

Pink decorator sugar crystals

Edible pink pearls and/or edible pink glitter

1 Heat oven to 350°F (325°F for dark or nonstick pans). Spray bottoms and sides of 2 (8- or 9-inch) round cake pans with baking spray with flour.

2 In large bowl, stir together cake mix and 1¼ cups champagne. Add oil, egg whites and food color; beat with electric mixer on medium speed 2 minutes. Pour into pans.

3 Bake as directed on box for 8- or 9-inch rounds. Cool 10 minutes. Remove from pans; place on cooling racks. Cool completely, about 1 hour.

4 In medium bowl, beat all frosting ingredients with electric mixer on medium speed until smooth. On serving plate, place 1 cake layer, rounded side down. Frost top of layer. Top with second layer, rounded side up. Frost side and top of cake. Sprinkle with garnishes. Store loosely covered.

1 Serving: Calories 460; Total Fat 15g (Saturated Fat 7g, Trans Fat 0g); Cholesterol 20mg; Sodium 340mg; Total Carbohydrate 72g (Dietary Fiber 0g); Protein 2g **Exchanges:** ½ Starch, 4½ Other Carbohydrate, 3 Fat **Carbohydrate Choices:** 5

Tip Sprinkle garnishes on the cake just before serving to maximize their sparkle and keep them from absorbing moisture and melting into the frosting.

Lemon Champagne Celebration Cupcakes

Prep Time: 40 Minutes • **Start to Finish:** 3 Hours 5 Minutes • Makes 12 servings

Cupcakes

1 box Betty Crocker SuperMoist yellow cake mix

½ cup water

½ cup dry champagne

½ cup vegetable oil

3 eggs

2 teaspoons grated lemon peel

Filling

¼ cup lemon curd (from 10-oz jar)

1 tablespoon sour cream

Icing

2 cups powdered sugar

2 tablespoons butter, melted

3 tablespoons fresh lemon juice

Garnish, if desired

Lemon peel curls

1. Heat oven to 350°F (325°F for dark or nonstick pan). Line 15 x 10 x 1-inch pan with foil. Spray with cooking spray.

2. Make cake batter as directed on box, using cake mix, water, champagne, oil and eggs. Stir 2 teaspoons grated lemon peel into batter. Pour into pan.

3. Bake 17 to 23 minutes or until toothpick inserted in center comes out clean. Do not remove cake from pan. Cool completely, about 1 hour. Place pan of cake in freezer. Freeze until firm, about 1 hour.

4. In small bowl, mix lemon curd and sour cream until well blended. Set aside.

5. To assemble cupcakes, remove cake from freezer; using foil, lift cake from pan. Using 2¼-inch round biscuit cutter, cut 24 rounds from cake. Place 12 rounds top side down. Spread each with about 1 teaspoon lemon curd filling. Top with remaining cake rounds, top side up.

6. In medium bowl, mix powdered sugar, melted butter and lemon juice until well blended. Spoon about 1 tablespoon icing over each cake, allowing icing to run down side of cake.

7. To serve, place each cake in decorative cupcake liner, and garnish with lemon peel curls.

1 Serving: Calories 270; Total Fat 11g (Saturated Fat 3g, Trans Fat 0g); Cholesterol 50mg; Sodium 220mg; Total Carbohydrate 41g (Dietary Fiber 0g); Protein 2g **Exchanges:** 1 Starch, 1½ Other Carbohydrate, 2 Fat **Carbohydrate Choices:** 3

Tip You'll find lemon curd in most large supermarkets with the preserves and jellies.

Chocolate-Fig Cake with Mascarpone Frosting

Prep Time: 30 Minutes • **Start to Finish:** 3 Hours 15 Minutes • Makes 16 servings

Cake

- 1 cup diced Calimyrna figs, stems removed (6 oz)
- 1 cup dry red wine (such as Merlot or Cabernet Sauvignon) or water
- 1 cup butter, softened
- 1 cup granulated sugar
- 2 eggs
- 1 teaspoon vanilla
- 1¾ cups Gold Medal® all-purpose flour
- 2 tablespoons unsweetened regular or dark baking cocoa
- 1 teaspoon baking soda
- 4 oz semisweet baking chocolate, melted, cooled

Frosting

- 1 container (8 oz) mascarpone cheese
- 2½ cups powdered sugar
- ½ teaspoon vanilla

Garnish, if desired

- 1 bar (1.55 oz) milk chocolate

1 Heat oven to 350°F. Grease bottom and side of 9- or 10-inch springform pan with shortening; lightly flour. In 1½-quart saucepan, combine figs and wine. Bring to a boil over medium-high heat. Remove from heat and cool while preparing batter.

2 In large bowl, beat butter and granulated sugar with electric mixer on medium speed until creamy. Add eggs and 1 teaspoon vanilla. Beat at medium speed until thick and creamy, scraping bowl occasionally. Add flour, cocoa and baking soda. Beat at low speed until moistened, scraping bowl occasionally. Add melted chocolate and the fig mixture. Beat at low speed until mixed. Spread in pan.

3 Bake 55 to 60 minutes or until toothpick inserted in center comes out clean. Cool in pan on cooling rack until completely cooled, about 2 hours. Remove side of pan.

4 In medium bowl, beat mascarpone cheese, powdered sugar and ½ teaspoon vanilla at low speed until mixed. Beat at medium speed until thick and creamy. Frost side and top of cake.

5 To make garnish, pull vegetable peeler along edges of chocolate bar to form curls. (If curls crumble, slightly warm chocolate bar with hand.) Garnish cake with chocolate curls. Store in refrigerator.

1 Serving: Calories 380; Total Fat 19g (Saturated Fat 12g, Trans Fat 0g); Cholesterol 65mg; Sodium 190mg; Total Carbohydrate 47g (Dietary Fiber 2g); Protein 3g **Exchanges:** 3 Other Carbohydrate, ½ Medium-Fat Meat, 3½ Fat **Carbohydrate Choices:** 3

Tip For large chocolate curls, melt 1½ ounces of semisweet baking chocolate with 1 teaspoon shortening. Spread on the back of a smooth baking sheet in 3 x 6-inch strip. Cool until set. Starting at one end, push flat metal spatula under chocolate to form ½-inch-wide curls.

Beer-licious Baking

Chocolate-Stout Caramel Corn

Prep Time: 35 Minutes • **Start to Finish:** 1 Hour 55 Minutes • Makes 14 servings (½ cup each)

8 cups popped popcorn

1 cup roasted salted almonds

½ cup stout beer

¼ cup packed brown sugar

¼ cup brown rice syrup or corn syrup

3 tablespoons butter

¼ teaspoon salt

1 cup chopped premium milk chocolate (6 oz)

1 Heat oven to 300°F. Line 2 (15 x 10 x 1-inch) pans with foil. Spray foil with cooking spray.

2 In large bowl, place popcorn and almonds; set aside.

3 In 2-quart saucepan, heat beer over medium heat, stirring frequently, about 6 minutes or until reduced to ¼ cup. Pour into glass measuring cup to confirm measure. Add back to saucepan. Stir in brown sugar, syrup and butter. Cook over medium heat, stirring occasionally, until bubbly around edges.

4 Reduce heat to medium-low; cook about 5 minutes longer, stirring occasionally, or until thickened and syrupy. Remove from heat; carefully stir in salt. Pour over popcorn mix in bowl; toss until evenly coated. Spread popcorn mixture in pans.

5 Bake 20 minutes, stirring every 5 minutes, to caramelize mixture. Cool completely, about 1 hour. Break into pieces; stir in chocolate. Store in tightly covered container.

1 Serving: Calories 230; Total Fat 14g (Saturated Fat 4.5g, Trans Fat 0g); Cholesterol 10mg; Sodium 110mg; Total Carbohydrate 21g (Dietary Fiber 2g); Protein 3g **Exchanges:** 1 Starch, ½ Other Carbohydrate, 2½ Fat **Carbohydrate Choices:** 1½

Tip Brown rice syrup is a sweetener derived from brown rice. It has mild malty notes that enhance the beer flavor in this recipe. It's available at large supermarkets or specialty shops.

Beer-and-Pretzel Chocolate Chip Cookies

Prep Time: 45 Minutes • **Start to Finish:** 1 Hour 45 Minutes • Makes 2 dozen cookies

Cookies

1 pouch (1 lb 1.5 oz) Betty Crocker chocolate chip cookie mix

½ cup butter, softened

1 egg

2 tablespoons stout beer

2 cups mini-pretzel twists, coarsely crushed

Frosting

½ cup whipping cream

2 tablespoons butter

5 oz semisweet baking chocolate, finely chopped

2 tablespoons stout beer

Topping

24 mini-pretzel twists

1 Heat oven to 375°F. In large bowl, stir cookie mix, ½ cup butter, the egg and 2 tablespoons beer until soft dough forms. Stir in crushed pretzels.

2 Drop dough by rounded tablespoonfuls onto ungreased cookie sheets 2 inches apart. Bake 9 to 11 minutes or until set. Cool 1 minute; remove from cookie sheets to cooling racks. Cool completely before frosting.

3 Meanwhile, in 1-quart saucepan, heat whipping cream and 2 tablespoons butter just to boiling over medium heat. Remove from heat and add chocolate; stir with whisk until melted and smooth. Stir in 2 tablespoons beer. Pour into small bowl; cover and refrigerate 1 to 2 hours or until spreading consistency.

4 Spread about 2 teaspoons frosting on each cookie; top each with 1 pretzel twist, pressing in gently. Store loosely covered.

1 Cookie: Calories 200; Total Fat 11g (Saturated Fat 6g, Trans Fat 0g); Cholesterol 25mg; Sodium 190mg; Total Carbohydrate 23g (Dietary Fiber 0g); Protein 2g **Exchanges:** ½ Starch, 1 Other Carbohydrate, 2 Fat **Carbohydrate Choices:** 1½

Tip For the best results, be sure to use real butter in the frosting.

Triple Chocolate–Stout Whoopie Pies

Prep Time: 45 Minutes • **Start to Finish:** 45 Minutes • Makes 20 whoopie pies

Cookies

- 1 box Betty Crocker SuperMoist devil's food cake mix
- ¼ cup unsweetened baking cocoa
- 1 box (4-serving size) chocolate instant pudding and pie filling mix
- ⅔ cup stout beer
- ½ cup vegetable oil
- 3 eggs

Filling

- 1 jar (7 oz) marshmallow creme (1½ cups)
- 1 cup butter, softened
- 1½ cups powdered sugar
- 2 tablespoons unsweetened baking cocoa
- 1 tablespoon stout beer
- ½ teaspoon vanilla

1 Heat oven to 350°F. Line cookie sheets with cooking parchment paper, or lightly spray with cooking spray.

2 In large bowl, beat all cookie ingredients with electric mixer on low speed until moistened; beat 1 minute longer on high speed. Drop batter by 2 tablespoonfuls 2 inches apart onto cookie sheets.

3 Bake 8 to 11 minutes or until set (do not overbake). Cool 2 minutes; remove from cookie sheets to cooling racks. Cool completely, about 15 minutes.

4 In large bowl, beat all filling ingredients with electric mixer on high speed until light and fluffy. For each whoopie pie, spread about 2 tablespoons filling on bottom of 1 cooled cookie. Top with second cookie, bottom side down. Store covered in refrigerator.

1 Whoopie Pie: Calories 320; Total Fat 17g (Saturated Fat 8g, Trans Fat 0g); Cholesterol 50mg; Sodium 350mg; Total Carbohydrate 40g (Dietary Fiber 1g); Protein 2g **Exchanges:** ½ Starch, 2 Other Carbohydrate, 3½ Fat **Carbohydrate Choices:** 2½

Tip For even more chocolate flavor, use a chocolate stout beer.

Tall, Dark and Stout Chocolate Layer Cake

Prep Time: 40 Minutes • **Start to Finish:** 3 Hours 30 Minutes • Makes 16 servings

Cake

- 1 box Betty Crocker SuperMoist devil's food cake mix
- 1¼ cups stout beer
- ⅓ cup vegetable oil
- 3 eggs

Frosting

- 12 oz semisweet baking chocolate, finely chopped
- 1½ cups whipping cream
- ½ cup butter

Filling

- 6 tablespoons caramel topping

1 Heat oven to 350°F (325°F for dark or nonstick pans). Grease bottoms only of 3 (9- or 8-inch) round cake pans. Make cake batter as directed on box, using cake mix, beer, oil and eggs. Divide batter evenly between pans, about 1½ cups batter each.

2 Bake 18 to 22 minutes or until toothpick inserted in center comes out clean. Cool 10 minutes. Remove from pans; place on cooling racks. Cool completely.

3 Meanwhile, place chocolate in medium bowl. In 2-quart saucepan, heat whipping cream and butter just to boiling over medium heat. Pour cream mixture over chocolate; stir with whisk until melted and smooth. Cover and refrigerate 1 hour; stir. Refrigerate 1 hour to 1 hour 30 minutes longer or until spreading consistency.

4 Place 1 cake layer on serving plate. Frost top of layer with 1 cup of the frosting. Drizzle with 3 tablespoons of the caramel topping. Top with second cake layer, 1 cup of the frosting and remaining 3 tablespoons caramel topping. Top with remaining cake layer and frosting.

1 Serving: Calories 420; Total Fat 26g (Saturated Fat 13g, Trans Fat 0.5g); Cholesterol 80mg; Sodium 320mg; Total Carbohydrate 42g (Dietary Fiber 2g); Protein 4g **Exchanges:** 1 Starch, 2 Other Carbohydrate, 5 Fat **Carbohydrate Choices:** 3

Salted Caramel, Stout and Chocolate Cheesecake

Prep Time: 15 Minutes • **Start to Finish:** 8 Hours 5 Minutes • Makes 16 servings

Crust
- 1 package (9 oz) thin chocolate wafer cookies, crushed (2 cups)
- 6 tablespoons butter or margarine, melted

Filling
- 2 packages (8 oz each) cream cheese, softened
- 2/3 cup granulated sugar
- 3 eggs
- 1 bag (12 oz) semisweet chocolate chips (2 cups), melted
- 1/4 cup whipping cream
- 3/4 cup stout beer
- 2 tablespoons butter or margarine, melted
- 1 teaspoon vanilla

Beer Sauce and Salt
- 1/2 cup butter
- 1 1/4 cups packed brown sugar
- 2 tablespoons stout beer
- 1/2 cup whipping cream
- 1 1/2 teaspoons sea salt flakes

1 Heat oven to 325°F. In medium bowl, mix all crust ingredients; reserve 1 tablespoon crumbs for garnish. Press remaining crumbs in bottom and 2 inches up side of ungreased 10-inch springform pan. Wrap outside bottom and side of pan with foil to prevent leaking. Refrigerate while making filling.

2 In large bowl, beat cream cheese and granulated sugar with electric mixer on medium speed until smooth. Beat in eggs, 1 at a time, until well blended, scraping bowl after each addition. Add melted chocolate; beat well. Add remaining filling ingredients; beat until smooth. Pour into crust-lined pan.

3 Bake 60 to 70 minutes or until edges are set; center of cheesecake will be soft. (To minimize cracking, place shallow pan half full of hot water on lower oven rack during baking.) Turn off oven; leave cheesecake in oven 30 minutes longer.

4 Without releasing side of pan, run knife around edge of pan to loosen cheesecake. Cool completely, about 2 hours. Refrigerate at least 4 hours or overnight.

5 In 2-quart saucepan, melt 1/2 cup butter over medium heat. Add brown sugar and 2 tablespoons stout beer. Heat to boiling; cook and stir about 1 minute or until sugar dissolves. Stir in 1/2 cup whipping cream; return to boiling. Remove from heat. Cool 10 minutes.

6 Run knife around edge of pan to loosen cheesecake again; carefully remove foil and side of pan. Cut cheesecake into slices. Drizzle sauce over slices; sprinkle with salt. Garnish with reserved crumbs. Cover and refrigerate any remaining cheesecake.

1 Serving: Calories 540; Total Fat 35g (Saturated Fat 20g, Trans Fat 1g); Cholesterol 115mg; Sodium 550mg; Total Carbohydrate 52g (Dietary Fiber 1g); Protein 5g **Exchanges:** 1 1/2 Starch, 2 Other Carbohydrate, 7 Fat **Carbohydrate Choices:** 3 1/2

Tip Don't worry about the center of the cheesecake being soft when you take it out of the oven. It becomes firm as it cools. To cut cheesecake easily, dip the knife into water and clean it off after every cut.

Bourbon Desserts

Boozy Bourbon-Chocolate Cupcakes

Prep Time: 40 Minutes • **Start to Finish:** 2 Hours 45 Minutes • Makes 24 cupcakes

1 Heat oven to 350°F (325°F for dark or nonstick pan). Generously spray 24 regular-size muffin cups with cooking spray. Make cake batter as directed on box, using cake mix, water, oil, bourbon, eggs and vanilla. Divide batter evenly among muffin cups, filling each about two-thirds full.

2 Bake 20 to 22 minutes or until toothpick inserted in center comes out clean. Cool 10 minutes; remove from pans to cooling racks. Cool completely, about 30 minutes.

3 Meanwhile, in medium microwavable bowl, microwave whipping cream uncovered on High 1 minute 30 seconds or until boiling. Stir in remaining filling ingredients until chocolate is melted and smooth. If necessary, microwave on High an additional 15 to 30 seconds until mixture can be stirred smooth. Cover; refrigerate about 1 hour or until spreading consistency.

4 In large bowl, beat marshmallow creme, 1 cup butter and the vodka with electric mixer on medium speed until blended. Beat in powdered sugar until fluffy. If necessary, beat in additional powdered sugar until piping consistency.

5 Cut cupcakes crosswise into halves. Spread about 1 tablespoon filling on each cupcake bottom; replace cupcake top. Pipe frosting on cupcake tops. Just before serving, drizzle each cupcake with ½ teaspoon coffee liqueur.

Cupcakes
- 1 box Betty Crocker SuperMoist devil's food cake mix
- 1 cup water
- ⅓ cup vegetable oil
- ¼ cup bourbon
- 3 eggs
- 1 teaspoon vanilla

Filling
- ¾ cup whipping cream
- 6 oz semisweet baking chocolate, finely chopped
- ⅓ cup butter, softened
- 3 tablespoons coffee liqueur

Frosting
- 1 jar (7 oz) marshmallow creme (1¾ cups)
- 1 cup butter, softened
- 2 tablespoons vanilla-flavored vodka
- 3 cups powdered sugar

Garnish
- ¼ cup coffee liqueur

1 Cupcake: Calories 340; Total Fat 19g (Saturated Fat 10g, Trans Fat 0g); Cholesterol 55mg; Sodium 230mg; Total Carbohydrate 38g (Dietary Fiber 1g); Protein 3g **Exchanges:** 1 Starch, 1½ Other Carbohydrate, 3½ Fat **Carbohydrate Choices:** 2½

Tip For the full tipsy effect, place each cupcake top at a slight angle.

Pecan-Bourbon Crunch Italian Cream Cups

Prep Time: 40 Minutes • **Start to Finish:** 1 Hour 40 Minutes • Makes 20 cupcakes

Cake
- 4 eggs
- ½ cup water
- 4½ teaspoons bourbon or apple cider
- 1 teaspoon vanilla
- 2¼ cups cake flour
- 1½ cups granulated sugar
- 2 teaspoons baking powder
- 1 bag (5 oz) glazed pecans, finely chopped
- 15 tablespoons butter or margarine, slightly softened
- 1 package (8 oz) cream cheese, softened

Frosting
- 9 tablespoons butter or margarine, slightly softened
- 2 tablespoons bourbon or apple cider
- ½ teaspoon finely grated lemon peel
- ⅛ teaspoon salt
- 4½ cups powdered sugar
- ¾ cup flaked coconut

1 Heat oven to 350°F. Place paper baking cup in each of 20 regular-size muffin cups.

2 In 2-cup glass measure, mix eggs, water, 4½ teaspoons bourbon and the vanilla with whisk. In medium bowl, mix flour, granulated sugar and baking powder. Remove 1 tablespoon of the flour mixture to small bowl; add ¾ cup of the glazed pecans and toss to coat. Set aside. Reserve remaining glazed pecans for frosting.

3 Cut butter into tablespoon-size pieces. Cut 3 tablespoons of the cream cheese into cubes; reserve remaining cream cheese for frosting. Add butter pieces and cream cheese cubes, a few at a time, to flour mixture, beating with electric mixer on low speed. Pour in all but ½ cup of the egg mixture. Beat on low speed 30 seconds, then medium speed 30 seconds, scraping bowl occasionally. Add remaining egg mixture in a slow stream; beat 30 seconds longer. Stir in reserved pecan mixture.

4 Divide batter evenly among muffin cups. Bake 20 to 25 minutes or until tops spring back when lightly touched. Cool 5 minutes; remove from pans to cooling racks. Cool completely, about 30 minutes.

5 Meanwhile, in large bowl, beat 9 tablespoons butter, 2 tablespoons bourbon, the lemon peel, salt and reserved cream cheese with electric mixer on low speed until smooth. Gradually beat in powdered sugar, 1 cup at a time, on low speed until smooth. Stir in ½ cup of the reserved glazed pecans and the coconut.

6 Pipe or spread frosting on top of each cupcake; sprinkle with remaining glazed pecans.

1 Cupcake: Calories 480; Total Fat 25g (Saturated Fat 13g, Trans Fat 0.5g); Cholesterol 90mg; Sodium 250mg; Total Carbohydrate 57g (Dietary Fiber 1g); Protein 4g **Exchanges:** 1½ Starch, 2½ Other Carbohydrate, 5 Fat **Carbohydrate Choices:** 4

Tip Lightly spray the lined muffin pan with cooking spray to help prevent the cupcake crowns from sticking to the pan.

Chocolate-Bourbon Pumpkin Cheesecake

Prep Time: 40 Minutes • **Start to Finish:** 9 Hours 35 Minutes • Makes 16 servings

Crust

2 cups gingersnap cookie crumbs (35 to 40 cookies)

¼ cup butter or margarine, melted

Cheesecake

4 packages (8 oz each) cream cheese, softened

1½ cups sugar

¼ cup Gold Medal all-purpose flour

4 eggs

4 tablespoons bourbon

½ cup canned pumpkin (not pumpkin pie mix)

1½ teaspoons aromatic bitters

1½ teaspoons ground ginger

1 teaspoon ground cinnamon

¼ teaspoon ground nutmeg

1 teaspoon vanilla

¾ cup semisweet chocolate chips, melted

Toppings

½ cup caramel topping

2 teaspoons bourbon

Dash aromatic bitters

Toasted pecans, if desired

1 Heat oven to 300°F. Grease 9-inch springform pan with shortening or cooking spray. Wrap outside bottom and side of pan with foil to prevent leaking. In small bowl, mix all crust ingredients. Press mixture in bottom and 1 inch up side of pan. Bake 8 to 10 minutes or until set. Cool 5 minutes.

2 In large bowl, beat cream cheese with electric mixer on medium speed just until smooth and creamy; do not overbeat. On low speed, gradually beat in sugar, then flour, then eggs one at a time, just until blended. Remove half of the cream cheese mixture (about 3 cups) into another large bowl; reserve.

3 Into remaining cream cheese mixture, stir 2 tablespoons of the bourbon, the pumpkin, 1½ teaspoons bitters, the ginger, cinnamon and nutmeg with whisk until smooth. Spoon over crust in pan. Into reserved 3 cups filling, stir remaining 2 tablespoons bourbon, the vanilla and melted chocolate; pour over pumpkin layer directly in middle of pan. This will create layers so that each slice includes some of each flavor.

4 To minimize cracking, place shallow pan half full of hot water on lower oven rack. Bake cheesecake 1 hour 20 minutes to 1 hour 30 minutes or until edges are set but center of cheesecake still jiggles slightly when moved.

5 Turn off oven; open oven door at least 4 inches. Leave cheesecake in oven 30 minutes longer. Remove from oven; place on cooling rack. Without releasing side of pan, run knife around edge of pan to loosen cheesecake. Cool 30 minutes. Cover loosely; refrigerate at least 6 hours but no longer than 24 hours.

6 Run knife around edge of pan to loosen cheesecake again; carefully remove foil and side of pan. Place cheesecake on serving plate. In small bowl, stir together caramel topping, 2 teaspoons bourbon and dash bitters. Drizzle with caramel and sprinkle with pecans. Cover and refrigerate any remaining cheesecake.

1 Serving: Calories 470; Total Fat 28g (Saturated Fat 15g, Trans Fat 1g); Cholesterol 115mg; Sodium 350mg; Total Carbohydrate 47g (Dietary Fiber 1g); Protein 7g **Exchanges:** 2½ Starch, ½ Other Carbohydrate, 5½ Fat **Carbohydrate Choices:** 3

Tip Bitters is an intensely flavored blend of aromatic herbs, barks, flowers, seeds and roots. It is used in small amounts to flavor cocktails or foods. It comes in a variety of flavors and can be found at most liquor stores.

Bourbon Brownie Bites with Dulce de Leche

Prep Time: 25 Minutes • **Start to Finish:** 1 Hour 30 Minutes • Makes 36 brownie bites

Brownie Bites

- 1 box (1 lb 5.2 oz) Betty Crocker Supreme triple chunk brownie mix
- ¼ cup vegetable oil
- ¼ cup bourbon
- 1 egg

Dulce de Leche

- 1 can (13.4 oz) dulce de leche (caramelized sweetened condensed milk)
- Coarse (kosher or sea) salt

1 Heat oven to 350°F (325°F for dark or nonstick pan). Place mini paper baking cup in each of 36 mini muffin cups. In medium bowl, stir all brownie ingredients until well blended. Divide batter evenly among muffin cups, filling each about three-fourths full.

2 Bake 14 to 16 minutes or until toothpick inserted in edge of brownie bite comes out clean. Do not overbake. Cool 10 minutes; remove from pan to cooling rack. Cool completely, about 30 minutes.

3 Top each brownie bite with dollop of dulce de leche; sprinkle with salt.

1 Brownie Bite: Calories 120; **Total Fat** 3.5g (Saturated Fat 1.5g, Trans Fat 0g); Cholesterol 10mg; Sodium 160mg; Total Carbohydrate 20g (Dietary Fiber 0g); Protein 1g **Exchanges:** ½ Starch, 1 Other Carbohydrate, ½ Fat **Carbohydrate Choices:** 1

Bourbon-Pecan Pie with Pecan Crust

Prep Time: 30 Minutes • **Start to Finish:** 4 Hours • Makes 8 servings

Crust
⅓ cup finely chopped pecans

2 tablespoons Gold Medal all-purpose flour

1 box refrigerated pie crusts, softened as directed on box

Filling
3 eggs

¾ cup packed brown sugar

3 tablespoons Gold Medal all-purpose flour

1 cup dark corn syrup

2 tablespoons butter or margarine, melted

2 tablespoons bourbon

1½ cups pecan halves

Topping
¾ cup whipping cream

2 tablespoons packed brown sugar

1 teaspoon vanilla

1 Heat oven to 325°F. In bottom of ungreased 9-inch glass pie plate, mix ⅓ cup chopped pecans and 2 tablespoons flour. Place pie crust over pecan mixture in pie plate as directed on box for One-Crust Filled Pie.

2 In large bowl, beat eggs slightly with hand beater or whisk. Beat in ¾ cup brown sugar, 3 tablespoons flour, the corn syrup, butter and bourbon until smooth. Stir in pecan halves. Pour into crust-lined pie plate.

3 Bake 15 minutes. Cover top of crust with foil to prevent excessive browning; bake 40 to 45 minutes longer or until filling is set and center of pie is puffed and golden brown. Cool completely on cooling rack, about 2 hours 30 minutes.

4 In chilled medium bowl, beat all topping ingredients with electric mixer on high speed until soft peaks form. Serve pie topped with whipped cream.

1 Serving: Calories 640; Total Fat 35g (Saturated Fat 11g, Trans Fat 0g); Cholesterol 115mg; Sodium 210mg; Total Carbohydrate 76g (Dietary Fiber 2g); Protein 6g **Exchanges:** 2½ Starch, 2½ Other Carbohydrate, 6½ Fat **Carbohydrate Choices:** 5

Tip Dark corn syrup has a caramel flavor and color added, which give it a darker color and stronger taste.

Rum-Tastic Treats

Rum-Glazed Spice Cocktail Cookies

Prep Time: 1 Hour • **Start to Finish:** 1 Hour 40 Minutes • Makes 66 cookies

Cookies

- 1 pouch (1 lb 1.5 oz) Betty Crocker sugar cookie mix
- 1/3 cup butter or margarine, melted
- 1/4 cup Gold Medal all-purpose flour
- 1 egg
- 1/2 teaspoon ground ginger
- 1/4 teaspoon ground allspice
- 1/4 teaspoon ground cinnamon
- 1/4 teaspoon ground cloves
- 1/4 teaspoon rum extract

Glaze and Topping

- 2 to 3 tablespoons milk
- 2 tablespoons dark rum or apple juice
- 2½ cups powdered sugar
- 3 tablespoons coarse sugar

1. Heat oven to 375°F. In medium bowl, stir all cookie ingredients until soft dough forms.

2. On floured surface, roll dough 1/8 inch thick. Cut with 2- to 2½-inch round cookie cutter. Reroll and cut remaining dough. On ungreased cookie sheets, place cutouts 1 inch apart.

3. Bake 7 to 9 minutes or until edges are set. Cool 1 minute; remove from cookie sheets to cooling racks. Cool completely, about 15 minutes.

4. In small bowl, stir 2 tablespoons of the milk, the rum and powdered sugar until smooth. Add additional milk, 1 teaspoon at a time, to desired consistency. Drizzle over cookies. Let stand until glaze is almost set; sprinkle with coarse sugar.

1 Cookie: Calories 60; Total Fat 1.5g (Saturated Fat 1g, Trans Fat 0g); Cholesterol 5mg; Sodium 30mg; Total Carbohydrate 11g (Dietary Fiber 0g); Protein 0g **Exchanges:** ½ Other Carbohydrate, ½ Fat **Carbohydrate Choices:** 1

Pecan-Rum Bars

Prep Time: 40 Minutes • **Start to Finish:** 2 Hours 15 Minutes • Makes 32 bars

Crust
1 cup butter, softened
1 cup packed brown sugar
2 cups Gold Medal all-purpose flour

Filling
2 eggs
½ cup packed brown sugar
½ cup dark corn syrup
1 tablespoon rum or 1 teaspoon rum extract
2 cups pecan halves

Icing
½ cup powdered sugar
1 tablespoon butter, softened
2 teaspoons rum or ½ teaspoon rum extract plus 2 teaspoons water

1 Heat oven to 375°F. Grease bottom and sides of 13 x 9-inch pan with shortening or cooking spray (do not use dark pan).

2 In medium bowl, beat 1 cup butter and 1 cup brown sugar with electric mixer on low speed until creamy. Stir in flour. Press evenly in pan.

3 Bake 12 to 14 minutes or until edges are golden brown and center springs back when touched lightly.

4 Meanwhile, in medium bowl, mix all filling ingredients except pecans. Stir in pecans. Pour over crust, spreading pecans evenly.

5 Bake 12 to 15 minutes or until filling is set. Cool completely, about 1 hour.

6 In small bowl, mix all icing ingredients (add additional rum or water, ½ teaspoon at a time, if icing is too thick to drizzle). Drizzle icing over bars. Cut into 8 rows by 4 rows.

1 Bar: Calories 200; Total Fat 11g (Saturated Fat 4.5g, Trans Fat 0g); Cholesterol 30mg; Sodium 55mg; Total Carbohydrate 23g (Dietary Fiber 0g); Protein 2g **Exchanges:** 1 Starch, ½ Other Carbohydrate, 2 Fat **Carbohydrate Choices:** 1½

Tip Create triangles by cutting each bar diagonally in half. And to keep bars longer, wrap tightly, label and freeze for up to 6 months.

Mojito Cake

Prep Time: 30 Minutes • **Start to Finish:** 2 Hours 20 Minutes • Makes 15 servings

1 Heat oven to 350°F (325°F for dark or nonstick pan). Spray bottom only of 13 x 9-inch pan with baking spray with flour.

2 In large bowl, beat all cake ingredients with electric mixer on low speed 30 seconds, then on medium speed 2 minutes, scraping bowl occasionally. Pour into pan.

3 Bake as directed on box for 13 x 9-inch pan. Cool 15 minutes.

4 Meanwhile, in 2-quart saucepan, mix all glaze ingredients. Heat to boiling over high heat, stirring frequently. Reduce heat to medium; continue to boil 3 minutes, stirring frequently, until glaze has thickened slightly.

5 Poke warm cake every inch with fork tines. Gradually pour glaze over cake. Cool completely, about 1 hour.

6 In small bowl, beat whipping cream and powdered sugar on high speed until soft peaks form. Top each serving with whipped cream and garnish with mint leaf and shredded lime peel. Store loosely covered.

Cake

- 1 box Betty Crocker SuperMoist white cake mix
- 1 cup unflavored carbonated water
- ⅓ cup vegetable oil
- ¼ cup rum or 1 teaspoon rum extract plus ¼ cup water
- 3 tablespoons chopped fresh mint leaves
- 2 teaspoons grated lime peel
- 3 egg whites

Glaze

- ½ cup butter or margarine
- ¼ cup water
- 1 cup granulated sugar
- ½ cup rum or 2 teaspoons rum extract plus ½ cup water

Garnish

- 1 cup whipping cream
- 2 tablespoons powdered sugar
- 15 fresh mint leaves, if desired
- Shredded lime peel, if desired

1 Serving: Calories 350; Total Fat 17g (Saturated Fat 8g, Trans Fat 0g); Cholesterol 35mg; Sodium 270mg; Total Carbohydrate 41g (Dietary Fiber 0g); Protein 2g **Exchanges:** ½ Starch, 2½ Other Carbohydrate, 3½ Fat **Carbohydrate Choices:** 3

Tip A mojito typically refers to a cocktail made with lime juice, sugar, mint leaves and rum. We've taken those same flavors and turned them into a tasty cake.

Chocolate Rum Cake

Prep Time: 15 Minutes • **Start to Finish:** 4 Hours • Makes 15 servings

Cake

1 box Betty Crocker SuperMoist devil's food or dark chocolate cake mix

1 cup water

⅓ cup vegetable oil

3 eggs

1 cup whipping cream

1 cup whole milk

1 can (14 oz) sweetened condensed milk

⅓ cup rum

Topping

1 cup whipping cream

2 tablespoons rum or 1 teaspoon rum extract

½ teaspoon vanilla

1 cup flaked coconut, toasted*

½ cup chopped pecans, toasted**

1 Heat oven to 350°F (325°F for dark or nonstick pan). Grease or spray bottom only of 13 x 9-inch pan.

2 In large bowl, beat cake mix, water, oil and eggs with electric mixer on low speed 30 seconds, then on medium speed 2 minutes. Pour into pan.

3 Bake 30 to 38 minutes or until toothpick inserted in center comes out clean. Let stand 5 minutes. In large bowl, mix 1 cup whipping cream, the whole milk, condensed milk and ⅓ cup rum. Pierce top of hot cake every ½ inch with long-tined fork, wiping fork occasionally to reduce sticking. Carefully pour whipping cream mixture evenly over top of cake. Cover and refrigerate about 3 hours or until chilled and most of whipping cream mixture has been absorbed into cake.

4 In chilled large bowl, beat 1 cup whipping cream, 2 tablespoons rum and the vanilla on high speed until soft peaks form. Frost cake with whipped cream mixture. Sprinkle with coconut and pecans. Store covered in refrigerator.

*To toast coconut, spread in ungreased shallow pan. Bake uncovered at 350°F 5 to 7 minutes, stirring occasionally, until golden brown.

**To toast pecans, spread in ungreased shallow pan. Bake uncovered at 350°F 6 to 10 minutes, stirring occasionally, until light brown.

1 Serving: Calories 430; Total Fat 24g (Saturated Fat 12g, Trans Fat 0g); Cholesterol 90mg; Sodium 330mg; Total Carbohydrate 43g (Dietary Fiber 1g); Protein 6g **Exchanges:** 1½ Starch, 1½ Other Carbohydrate, 4½ Fat **Carbohydrate Choices:** 3

Tip Instead of rum in the cake, use 1 tablespoon rum extract plus enough water to measure ⅓ cup. In the topping, substitute 1 teaspoon rum extract for the rum.

Hot Buttered Rum Cheesecake with Brown Sugar–Rum Sauce

Prep Time: 45 Minutes • **Start to Finish:** 15 Hours 20 Minutes • Makes 16 servings

Crust
1¼ cups graham cracker crumbs
¼ cup butter or margarine, melted

Filling
5 packages (8 oz each) cream cheese, softened
1¼ cups granulated sugar
⅓ cup whipping cream
2 tablespoons rum
¼ teaspoon ground cinnamon
⅛ teaspoon ground cloves
⅛ teaspoon ground nutmeg
3 eggs

Sauce
½ cup packed brown sugar
¼ cup butter or margarine
⅓ cup whipping cream
¼ cup rum
¼ cup golden raisins, if desired

1 Heat oven to 350°F. In small bowl, mix all crust ingredients. Press firmly in bottom of ungreased 9-inch springform pan. Wrap outside bottom and side of pan with foil to prevent leaking. Bake 10 minutes. Cool completely. Reduce oven temperature to 325°F.

2 Meanwhile, in large bowl, beat all filling ingredients except eggs with electric mixer on medium speed about 1 minute or until smooth. On low speed, beat in eggs until well blended. Pour over crust; smooth top.

3 Bake 1 hour 15 minutes to 1 hour 25 minutes or until edge is set and center is still soft. Turn off oven; open oven door at least 4 inches. Leave cheesecake in oven 30 minutes. Remove from oven; cool in pan on cooling rack away from drafts 30 minutes.

4 Without releasing side of pan, run knife around edge of pan to loosen cheesecake. Refrigerate uncovered about 3 hours or until chilled. Cover; continue refrigerating at least 9 hours but no longer than 48 hours.

5 In 1½-quart saucepan, mix all sauce ingredients. Heat to boiling over medium heat, stirring constantly. Boil 3 to 4 minutes, stirring constantly, until slightly thickened.

6 Run knife around edge of pan to loosen cheesecake again; carefully remove foil and side of pan. Serve with warm sauce. Store cheesecake and sauce covered in refrigerator.

1 Serving: Calories 470; Total Fat 35g (Saturated Fat 22g, Trans Fat 1.5g); Cholesterol 145mg; Sodium 300mg; Total Carbohydrate 30g (Dietary Fiber 0g); Protein 7g **Exchanges:** 2 Other Carbohydrate, 1 High-Fat Meat, 5½ Fat **Carbohydrate Choices:** 2

Pear-Rum Crisp

Prep Time: 20 Minutes • **Start to Finish:** 1 Hour 5 Minutes • Makes 6 servings

Fruit Mixture

- ½ cup packed brown sugar
- 3 tablespoons Gold Medal all-purpose flour
- ½ teaspoon ground cinnamon
- ½ teaspoon ground nutmeg
- 3 firm ripe medium pears, peeled, sliced (6 cups)
- ¼ cup sweetened dried cranberries
- ¼ cup dark rum, apple juice or apple cider

Topping

- ½ cup Gold Medal all-purpose flour
- ½ cup packed brown sugar
- ½ teaspoon ground cinnamon
- ½ cup cold butter or margarine
- ½ cup quick-cooking oats

1 Heat oven to 350°F. Grease bottom and sides of 8-inch square (2-quart) glass baking dish with butter or cooking spray.

2 In large bowl, stir ½ cup brown sugar, 3 tablespoons flour, ½ teaspoon cinnamon and the nutmeg until mixed. Add pears, cranberries and rum; stir to coat fruit with sugar mixture. Spread in baking dish.

3 In medium bowl, mix ½ cup flour, ½ cup brown sugar and ½ teaspoon cinnamon. Cut in butter, using pastry blender or fork, until mixture looks like fine crumbs. Add oats; stir until crumbly. Sprinkle evenly over fruit mixture.

4 Bake 40 to 45 minutes or until pears are tender when pierced with fork and topping is golden brown. Serve warm or at room temperature.

1 Serving: Calories 470; Total Fat 16g (Saturated Fat 10g, Trans Fat 0.5g); Cholesterol 40mg; Sodium 125mg; Total Carbohydrate 77g (Dietary Fiber 6g); Protein 3g **Exchanges:** 1 Starch, 1 Fruit, 3 Other Carbohydrate, 3 Fat **Carbohydrate Choices:** 5

Tip   For a flavor twist, add ¼ cup raisins to the fruit mixture.

Metric Conversion Guide

Volume

U.S. Units	Canadian Metric	Australian Metric
¼ teaspoon	1 mL	1 ml
½ teaspoon	2 mL	2 ml
1 teaspoon	5 mL	5 ml
1 tablespoon	15 mL	20 ml
¼ cup	50 mL	60 ml
⅓ cup	75 mL	80 ml
½ cup	125 mL	125 ml
⅔ cup	150 mL	170 ml
¾ cup	175 mL	190 ml
1 cup	250 mL	250 ml
1 quart	1 liter	1 liter
1½ quarts	1.5 liters	1.5 liters
2 quarts	2 liters	2 liters
2½ quarts	2.5 liters	2.5 liters
3 quarts	3 liters	3 liters
4 quarts	4 liters	4 liters

Weight

U.S. Units	Canadian Metric	Australian Metric
1 ounce	30 grams	30 grams
2 ounces	55 grams	60 grams
3 ounces	85 grams	90 grams
4 ounces (¼ pound)	115 grams	125 grams
8 ounces (½ pound)	225 grams	225 grams
16 ounces (1 pound)	455 grams	500 grams
1 pound	455 grams	0.5 kilogram

Note: The recipes in this cookbook have not been developed or tested using metric measures. When converting recipes to metric, some variations in quality may be noted.

Measurements

Inches	Centimeters
1	2.5
2	5.0
3	7.5
4	10.0
5	12.5
6	15.0
7	17.5
8	20.5
9	23.0
10	25.5
11	28.0
12	30.5
13	33.0

Temperatures

Fahrenheit	Celsius
32°	0°
212°	100°
250°	120°
275°	140°
300°	150°
325°	160°
350°	180°
375°	190°
400°	200°
425°	220°
450°	230°
475°	240°
500°	260°

Recipe Testing and Calculating Nutrition Information

Recipe Testing:

- Large eggs and 2% milk were used unless otherwise indicated.
- Fat-free, low-fat, low-sodium or lite products were not used unless indicated.
- No nonstick cookware and bakeware were used unless otherwise indicated. No dark-colored, black or insulated bakeware was used.
- When a pan is specified, a metal pan was used; a baking dish or pie plate means ovenproof glass was used.
- An electric hand mixer was used for mixing only when mixer speeds are specified.

Calculating Nutrition:

- The first ingredient was used wherever a choice is given, such as ⅓ cup sour cream or plain yogurt.
- The first amount was used wherever a range is given, such as 3- to 3½-pound whole chicken.
- The first serving number was used wherever a range is given, such as 4 to 6 servings.
- "If desired" ingredients were not included.
- Only the amount of a marinade or frying oil that is absorbed was included.

America's most trusted cookbook is better than ever!

- 1,100 all-new photos, including hundreds of step-by-step images
- More than 1,500 recipes, with hundreds of inspiring variations and creative "mini" recipes for easy cooking ideas
- Brand-new features
- Gorgeous new design

Get the best edition of the *Betty Crocker Cookbook* today!

www.ingramcontent.com/pod-product-compliance
Lightning Source LLC
Chambersburg PA
CBHW071417290426
44108CB00014B/1871